DISCARD

Written by Kathy Schulz
Illustrated by Katherine Potter

Children's Press®
A Division of Scholastic Inc.
New York • Toronto • London • Auckland • Sydney
Mexico City • New Delhi • Hong Kong
Danbury, Connecticut

To my teaching colleagues
who work so hard to keep children safe
—K.S.

For Julia and Rachel
—K.P.

Reading Consultants
Linda Cornwell
Literacy Specialist

Katharine A. Kane
Education Consultant
(Retired, San Diego County Office of Education and San Diego State University)

Library of Congress Cataloging-in-Publication Data

Schulz, Kathy.
  Always be safe / written by Kathy Schulz ; illustrated by Katherine Potter.
      p. cm. — (Rookie reader)
Summary: A rhyming review of some basic safety tips.
  ISBN 0-516-22594-4 (lib. bdg.)   0-516-26965-8 (pbk.)
  1. Safety education—Juvenile literature. 2. Children's accidents—Prevention—
Juvenile literature. [1. Safety.] I. Potter, Katherine, ill. II. Title. III. Series.
  HQ770.7 S34 2003
  613.6'071—dc21
                            2002008783

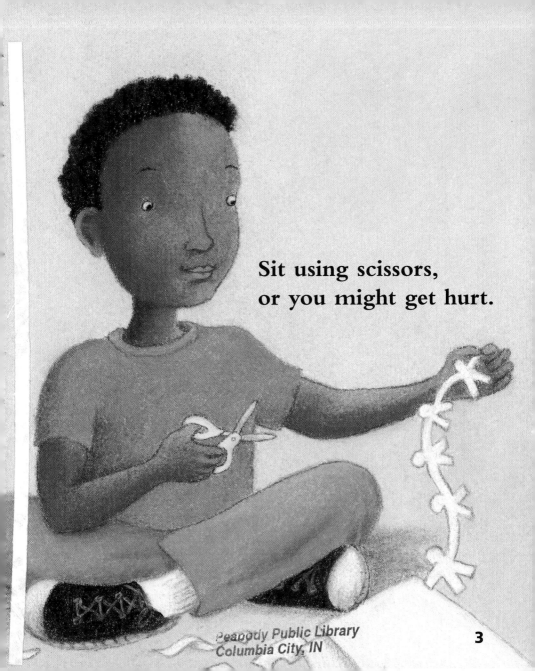

Sit using scissors,
or you might get hurt.

3

Wash before eating,
or you might eat dirt!

Ask before tasting,
or you might get sick.

6

Check before touching,
or you just might stick!

Stay with a grown-up,
or you might get lost.

Sit in your chair right,
or you might get tossed!

Hold on while climbing,
or you might fall off.

Zip up your coat,
or you might
start to cough.

Ask before petting,
or you might get nipped.

Tie before walking,
or you might be tripped.

Ride with a helmet,
or you might get lumps.

Buckle your seatbelt,
or you might get bumps.

Always be safe...

in whatever you do.

Nothing is quite
as important as you.

Word List (63 words)

a	dirt	just	safe	tripped
always	do	lost	scissors	up
as	eat	lumps	seatbelt	using
ask	eating	might	sick	walking
be	fall	nipped	sit	wash
before	get	nothing	start	whatever
buckle	grown-up	off	stay	while
bumps	helmet	on	stick	with
chair	hold	or	tasting	you
check	hurt	petting	tie	your
climbing	important	quite	to	zip
coat	in	ride	tossed	
cough	is	right	touching	

About the Author

As an elementary school teacher, Kathy Schulz has spent a lot of time teaching children about being safe. She hopes that *Always Be Safe* will serve as a reminder to children that safety is very important . . . and so are they. When she is not teaching, writing, or volunteering at an animal shelter, Kathy enjoys taking walks with her dog. (She uses a leash to be sure that Baxter will always be safe, too.)

About the Illustrator

Katherine Potter has illustrated six books for children, two of which she also wrote. When her two daughters, husband, and dog Arlo are not keeping her busy, she likes to draw, listen to music, and play the piano.